Lent

ONE DAY AT A TIME FOR CATHOLIC TEENS

Katie Prejean McGrady & Tommy McGrady

AVE MARIA PRESS AVE Notre Dame, Indiana

To our Rose,
the light of our lives and joy of our hearts.
We love you, bud.

———————————————————————

Founded in 1865, Ave Maria Press is a ministry of the United States Province of Holy Cross.

www.avemariapress.com

Paperback: ISBN-13 978-1-59471-908-0

E-book: ISBN-13 978-1-59471-909-7

Cover and text design by Samantha Watson.

Printed and bound in the United States of America.

Introduction

What makes the desert beautiful . . . is that somewhere it
hides a well.
—Antoine de Saint-Exupéry, *The Little Prince*

Students rushed in as the tardy bell rang, sliding into their desks and grabbing pen and paper to answer the journal prompt written on the whiteboard. I (Katie) checked attendance and let them work quietly as they answered the day's question: "Why do you think Lent is forty days long?"

As they worked, I pulled up the lecture notes and presentation on my computer and waited patiently, watching as pens were set down one by one, students turning to visit with their friends when they finished.

"That's it . . . Lent is RUINED!"

Scanning the room, I noticed right away who had shouted in frustration. In the back row, with a candy bar wrapper in his hand, sat Gus: a jovial kid who played football, served on student council, and filled the role of lovable class clown most days.

"Did you give up candy for Lent, Gus?" I asked, chuckling quietly.

"YEAH! And I TOTALLY FORGOT!" he said, in between chews. "Gabe just handed this to me and I ate it without thinking and now . . ." his words trailed off as he took another big bite of the forbidden candy bar, "and now, Lent is OVER! I didn't even last a week."

Have you ever made that same mistake? Lent starts on Ash Wednesday, and, just like a New Year's resolution, you set a lofty goal for yourself to not eat candy or to avoid sodas or to pray a Rosary every day or to become a super-awesome-saintly-holy-best-Catholic-ever. . . . And inevitably, a few days into Lent, something happens: you instinctively grab a piece of candy from a dish, or you buy a soda at lunch, or you totally forget to pray the Rosary before you go to bed, and next thing you know, it's the week before Easter and you haven't done anything you wanted to do or not do the entire season of Lent and you think that Lent is just completely ruined.

If we think about Lent as a season of "doing this" or "not doing that," then it's very easy to fail. When we pigeonhole the entire season as a time to complete our Catholic to-do lists filled with stressful tasks, it's easy to treat these forty days with a win-or-lose attitude. Either we successfully give up the one thing we like and we have a good Lent, *or* we fail miserably and give in to a temptation and the entire season becomes a colossal waste of time.

When we think of Lent only in these black-and-white terms and make it about the external things we do or don't do, then it becomes a few weeks of hurrying up and getting to Easter so we can get back all that stuff we gave up and take a rest from all that extra holy stuff we tried to cram in and celebrate Easter, with marshmallow chicks and fine chocolates. With this little book we want to help you break that cycle of lame Lents and instead take you on a journey of sorts that we hope brings you closer to Jesus.

Rather than doing a half-hearted Lent this year, what if you approach it as a time that can center and reshape your entire year, maybe even your whole life? What if you enter into the spiritual desert of Lent ready to seek out and meet Jesus—person-to-person? What if Lent is forty days *in* and *through* the desert, and while there, you have an authentic, personal, life-changing encounter with the living God? What if Lent is a chance for you to pray daily, make meaningful sacrifices, and seek opportunities to serve those around you?

Lent isn't just forty sequential days with extra spiritual things to do. It's meant to be a time of true conversion, when you walk through the desert and come out on the other side having met Jesus, ready to continue growing in relationship with him as you contemplate the meaning of his death and resurrection for your own life.

If we really do believe Lent should shape and form our whole year, and it is not just these forty days that get us to jelly beans and chocolate bunnies, pastel colors and egg hunts, an empty tomb and *Alleluia*, then we have to walk through the Lenten desert with purpose, focus, and a real desire to meet Jesus and be changed by him. This little book is your guide and companion for that journey.

Using this Booklet

First things first: You will want to keep a Bible and a notepad or journal nearby when using this booklet. (The scripture quotations in this booklet are from the *New American Bible, Revised Edition*.)

Each Sunday, we'll give you three simple challenges based on a passage from one of the gospels to direct you through the week. You'll focus on building your prayer life, making intentional sacrifices, and giving of yourself in some way. We've built in room for you to make some notes or write your goals for the week.

Monday through Friday, you'll read a short reflection on a passage from scripture, usually the Psalms, and you'll be challenged to think about something very specific or do something to help unpack the day's verse. If you can, try to read the reflections and challenges in the morning, so you can think about them throughout the coming day. These challenges and questions are a chance to examine what's going on in your life, how you're approaching and encountering Jesus, and how you're being formed, one day at a time, into a person who is truly transformed by the Lord.

To wrap up each week, on Saturdays we'll give you three deep-dive questions to help you reflect on the week you just had. Hopefully, thinking through these questions will show you Christ active in the week gone by, prepare you for the next week, and draw you closer to the living God.

With *Lent: One Day at a Time for Catholic Teens*, you have everything you need to journey through Lent. You can focus on these forty days as a time to stretch and grow as you keep your eyes fixed on Jesus and deepen your relationship with him, and be truly transformed by, and in, this Lenten desert.

Ash Wednesday

And your Father who sees **in secret** will repay you.
—Matthew 6:4

Today Catholics around the world go to church and receive black crosses on their foreheads. In Matthew's gospel, Jesus says that we shouldn't do good deeds, give to the poor, or pray so that others notice. Rather, we should do these things quietly, or "in secret." Does walking around all day with ashes on our foreheads contradict what Jesus wants from us?

If you have ashes on your forehead today, don't worry. When Jesus says to do things of faith quietly, he's talking about the importance of our inner lives. He reminds us that God is watching, and sees what others don't. He knows what's in our hearts.

Pick a Challenge for this Week

- Write an encouraging or affirming note to someone anonymously.
- Post a prayer or reflection about your Lenten journey on social media and don't track likes, shares, or retweets.
- Do one of your siblings' chores or a household task/project that your parents normally take care of without telling them.

Feel Ambitious?

Read Matthew 6:1–21 and write a brief note to Jesus giving your plans for Lent. Try three things to match the three disciplines of Lent: prayer, fasting, and almsgiving.

Closing Prayer

Jesus, draw me close to you these forty days.
Let me seek you with focus.
Cleanse me of my pride.
Help me look to you alone,
and give me strength to love others as you do.
Amen.

Thursday after Ash Wednesday

To you I raise my eyes,
to you enthroned in heaven.
—Psalm 123:1

This Lenten journey through the desert with Jesus has just begun, but this is not *your* beginning. You have been on a journey since the day you were born. You've learned lots of lessons, made a few mistakes, established habits (both good and bad), and taken on burdens that may sometimes feel like they are too much to bear.

As you walk through the desert, there will be moments when you become more aware of who you are and see all that you've learned and where you need to grow. In these moments, it's important to look to Jesus, and remember he is with you on this journey. You are not alone in the desert. And when you lift your eyes, you will see that Jesus is walking with you, reminding you that he's already won victory over sin and death.

Grow Your Soul

Write about a struggle you have had to overcome. Ask yourself: How did I make it through? Who helped me along the way?

Feel Ambitious?

Read Psalm 123 and spend some time in quiet meditation, pondering the Lord's goodness. If you're able, go pray at an adoration chapel or an open church for a few minutes today.

Closing Prayer

Jesus, I am often weighed down by the burdens I carry.
I am distracted by the struggles I face.
Help me to keep my eyes fixed on you,
so that I may share in your glory. Amen.

Friday after Ash Wednesday

Have mercy on me, God,
in accord with your **merciful love**.
—Psalm 51:3

It's the third day of Lent. Maybe you've already indulged in what you promised to give up, or kept to yourself what you promised to give away, or maybe you accidentally ate meat on this first Friday of Lent.

Lapses in judgment or memory can lead us to think, "Oh well, maybe next year!" or even worse, "If I don't run to Confession, I'm going to hell!" If one of these reactions sounds like you, stop! Take a breath and read the line of scripture at the top of this page again.

God is not waiting for us to screw up so he can smack us down. When we fall short, God does not look at us with disappointment, anger, or vengeance. Rather, he looks at us with the gentleness of a father whose child is hurt; he swoops in, picks her up, and kisses what hurts. Turn to our heavenly Father today and accept his healing touch.

Grow Your Soul

Think of a moment when you fell short of being the person you want to be, and ask God for the grace to look at yourself with *his* gentleness.

Feel Ambitious?

Read Psalm 51. Write down as many interactions with your friends, teachers, and parents that you can remember from the last twenty-four hours. As you think about those moments, ask Jesus for help being gentle with yourself, and merciful toward others.

Closing Prayer

Jesus, I am often my own worst critic.
Help me to see myself as you do,
and allow me to also see others through your eyes.
Amen.

Saturday after Ash Wednesday

Lord, you are good and forgiving,
most merciful to all who call on you.
—Psalm 86:5

Giving up or fasting from something during Lent can make us cranky. Something as simple as your mom reminding you of a chore you forgot, or the homework you've put off, can push you over the proverbial edge. Or perhaps it's your sister droning on about the latest drama in her life. It may even be your best friend smacking his gum or annoying you with some other irritating habit. Some pet peeve gets under your skin, and suddenly you lose control and say something snarky to your unsuspecting loved one.

In this season of Lent, when tensions can run high as we move from being attached to certain things to giving those things up so we can focus on Jesus, it may be helpful to recall the reason we are doing all of this. We sacrifice (give something up or fast) not so that we can show off how good we are; we sacrifice so that we may better imitate Jesus in all that we say and in all that we do. He is good, forgiving, and merciful to all who turn to him, and we are called to be the same.

This Week's Wins

- Looking back on these first few days of Lent, in what ways have you stayed true to the sacrifices and fasting you promised?

- When did you set aside time for prayer or serving others? How did it feel to focus on talking to God?

- What small service did you do for someone else? Write about what that was like.

Feel Ambitious?

Read Psalm 86 and write down moments from the last few days when you felt anxious, frustrated, or stressed. Who did you take it out on? Pray for that person, then go and apologize.

Closing Prayer

Jesus, sometimes I am the least loving to those I love most.
Give me patience and peace to respond as you would.
Help me see myself and others as you do: with eyes of mercy and love.
Amen.

First Sunday of Lent
ENTER IN

Filled with the holy Spirit, Jesus returned from the Jordan
and was led by the Spirit **into the desert** for forty days.
—Luke 4:1–2

The desert isn't a very inviting place for most humans. It's where things shrivel up and often die. Water and vegetation are dangerously scarce. The blazing sun beats down all day, and at night it's freezing cold. But it's a desert that Jesus enters right after he's baptized. In fact, he's driven there by the Holy Spirit so that he can pray, fast, think, and prepare.

Jesus goes to a place most of us avoid so that he can be transformed and get ready for the years of his public ministry. In order to preach, heal, teach, and eventually die on the Cross, Jesus takes forty days in the desert to prepare for his mission. You and I are called to do the same.

You are being prepared for something this Lent, and the Lord is going to work on your heart, mind, and soul over these days. Incredible things can happen if you join Jesus in the desert: you can learn to trust him more, surrendering your worries and fears; you can rest in his tender mercy and love. Let Jesus lead you. As this first full week of Lent begins, enter the stillness of the desert and welcome the Spirit, who will lead you to Jesus.

Pick a Challenge for this Week

- Ask Jesus to show you how he wants you to grow this Lent. Then ask yourself: What may be holding me back today from entering the desert to walk with Jesus? Pray that you can let whatever it is go.

- Each day, give up one food or drink item that you really enjoy so that you're reminded of the dryness of the desert, where you will find Jesus. Make a list of what you will give up each day.

- Each evening, thank God for one good thing that happened during your day and tell Jesus how you will be different because of that gift.

Feel Ambitious?

Read Luke 4:1–13 and write a short note or a letter to Jesus, telling him about the things that tempt you away from doing what is right. Share with him your worries and ask for his help.

Closing Prayer

Jesus, help me enter the desert with an open mind,
a ready heart, and a trusting spirit.
Show me where I need to grow,
and lead me where you need me to be. Amen.

First Monday of Lent

To you, O Lord, I lift up my soul,
my God, in you **I trust**.
—Psalm 25:1

Most of us really like control. We like deciding where we go, who we spend time with, and what we watch on TV. We like to call most of the shots about how we spend our money and what we do with our free time. We strive to be in charge.

But, when we're busy controlling things, we leave little room for surprises. Sometimes we leave little room for welcoming other people in and getting to know them. This is especially true when it comes to befriending Jesus. If you really want to wander in this Lenten desert and allow yourself to be led by the Spirit and to trust, you have to surrender. Lift your heart, mind, and soul to the Lord today, so that you can pay attention to where he might be leading you. Trust that he knows what is best.

Grow Your Soul

Name three things you like to control. Do you trust Jesus to affect these things? Who or what has taught you to trust? Why do you sometimes struggle with trust?

Feel Ambitious?

Read Psalm 25:1–9, then sit in silent contemplation before the Lord, who is good and upright. Place one of the items from your list in God's merciful hands. Let go.

Closing Prayer

Jesus, help me trust you more,
especially as I walk through the Lenten desert.
Give me strength to lift my heart, mind, and soul to you
and be open to your guidance. Amen.

First Tuesday of Lent

I sought the Lord, and he answered me,
delivered me from all my fears.
—Psalm 34:5

We're all scared of something. It might be spiders, the dark, failure, or being alone. We might be scared of being left out, or of being noticed. Some people are scared of the future, while others are scared of the past. We're all scared, and sometimes we let our fears cripple us.

Walking through the desert and trusting the Lord can be scary too. Not knowing how Jesus might change you may make you fearful and shut you down, preventing you from continuing on your Lenten journey toward a deeper spiritual life.

Instead of letting fear take control, try offering your fears to Jesus. When you're scared of the future or of being left out, seek the Lord's guidance. Ask him to give you strength and courage, and listen for his voice. Let Jesus deliver you from your fears.

Grow Your Soul

Name one thing that scares you. Why does it scare you? What can you do with the help of Jesus to transform that fear into strength?

Feel Ambitious?

Read Psalm 34:2–7. Think about a time when you were delivered from distress and offer God praise and thanksgiving for this great gift.

Closing Prayer

Jesus, be with me.
When I'm nervous, comfort me.
When I'm unsure, guide me.
When I'm afraid, deliver me.
Help me to always cling to you.
Amen.

First Wednesday of Lent

A clean heart create for me, God;
renew within me a steadfast spirit.
—Psalm 51:12

We know when something is clean—it smells nice, it's neat and tidy, it looks bright and shiny. And we definitely know when something is not clean—it might have a funny smell, maybe it's cluttered and gross, it looks dingy. Sometimes our hearts are clean, and sometimes they're not. But no matter what, Jesus wants a relationship with us, and he loves us completely whether we're cluttered and dingy or bright and shiny.

We enter into the Lenten desert *hoping* that our hearts will be cleansed, become reordered and refocused on what really matters. That's what it means to have a clean heart. It's a heart that's confident in God's love for us and our love of God. It's a heart focused on how God wants us to live.

Grow Your Soul

Pause to take note of all the dingy, cluttered parts of your heart. How might these things keep you away from Jesus? What will you do to tidy up your life and focus instead on living in friendship with Christ?

Feel Ambitious?

Read Psalm 51:3–15, then sit in silent praise of God for the ever-present gift of forgiveness.

Closing Prayer

Jesus, I want to focus on you.
I want to love you with all that I am.
Cleanse my heart and draw it close to yours.
Amen.

First Thursday of Lent

Though I walk in the midst of dangers,
you guard my life when my enemies rage.
You stretch out your hand.
—Psalm 138:7

You can be confident that Jesus will guard you and his love will catch you whenever you stumble. You might stumble over a broken Lenten promise to do more for the poor or to pray each night. Or you might stumble in your relationship with your mom or dad because of hurt feelings or anger. Whatever the stumble, look for help in Jesus.

The road toward joy and union with Christ is long, filled with detours and potholes and far too many chances to wander off. These can slow your journey and keep you from real change. And that's precisely when you need Jesus the most.

You are never alone in the desert, wandering aimlessly. Jesus is right there, guarding your life, guiding your steps, and stretching out his hand.

Grow Your Soul

Identify a danger you face as you try to grow in your faith at school, in your home, or with your friends. What is really challenging about this danger, and why could it draw you away from Jesus?

Feel Ambitious?

Read Psalm 138:1–8 and then identify a few moments when you believe God was protecting you from some danger or harm. How do you want to respond to that gift?

Closing Prayer

Jesus, I walk in the midst of dangers,
but I know you are here.
Catch me when I stumble.
Draw me near to you. Amen.

First Friday of Lent

Out of the depths I call to you, Lord;
Lord, hear my cry!
—Psalm 130:1–2

Have you ever sent a text and received no immediate response? Longer than an hour, and it gets annoying. Longer than a day, and it's maddening, right? Longer than a week—well, it's like you're not even friends anymore! It's like they didn't hear you, and when you're not heard, it hurts. Sometimes, it can feel the same with prayer. We pray and hope God hears. But prayers don't have read receipts

You may feel at times like you're crying out and no one is there. But Jesus is right there, walking beside you, listening to you, attentive to your every cry. Lent is a good time to call out to him, place your trust in him, and let him love you.

Grow Your Soul

Spend five minutes in quiet prayer and make a list of three things you distinctly want to say to the Lord. Be specific and personal.

1.
2.
3.

Feel Ambitious?

Read all of Psalm 130 and take a moment to speak to the Lord from your heart. Write your prayer out and look at it throughout the day.

Closing Prayer

Jesus, give me confidence in your attentive heart.
I want to cry out to you and trust that you hear me.
Strengthen my trust. Amen.

First Saturday of Lent

He will be your God, and **you will walk in his ways**,
observe his statutes, commandments, and ordinances, and
obey his voice.
—Deuteronomy 26:17

We live in a noisy world. So much calls for our attention: phones and the internet, unlimited access to entertainment, the never-ending stream of social media notifications. It's tough to stay focused on, much less fully *enter into*, the Lenten desert for forty days and concentrate on meeting Jesus. It's hard to let ourselves be changed as we grow in relationship with him.

But that's what we're called to do, both during Lent and every day after. Jesus invites us to walk along with him and be willing to change. He asks us to trust him, especially as he points us to his Father, *our* Father, who has good plans for us, delivers us from our fears, and calls us to be transformed by his love. Jesus asks us to fully enter into the desert so we can be completely and totally his.

This isn't easy, and surrendering your control certainly won't happen overnight. But, bit by bit, as you make this Lenten journey, let yourself trust Jesus more and more. Learn to walk in his ways, pay attention to his guidance, and listen for his voice.

This Week's Wins

- Think back on your week. What are three Lenten things you did well?

- What three things are you most grateful for at the end of this week?

- How is your life better today because of Jesus?

Feel Ambitious?

Read Deuteronomy 26:16–19. Then write a letter to your future self, describing how you grew closer to Jesus this week and what you've learned about the Father.

Closing Prayer

Jesus, thank you for the chance to follow you.
Guide me as I walk through the Lenten desert with you,
and help me remember how much you love me.
Amen.

Second Sunday of Lent
SEE AND BE SEEN

Peter and his companions had been overcome by sleep,
but **becoming fully awake, they saw his glory**.
—Luke 9:32

We *see* a lot during the day. We stare at screens, read books, look at other people. Sight guides us, and the things we look at affect what we do. You see a text—you respond. You watch a favorite sitcom—you laugh. You see a red light—you stop. Even the most ordinary, boring things that we see influence us.

So, what happens when we see something incredible—say, God in all his divine glory? Now, that's life-changing! Everything is different after that.

Where might you see the glory of God? Consider your day-to-day existence. The sun rises, and you see God's creative beauty in the colors cast across the sky. A friend makes you laugh, and the joy shared is a reminder of God's goodness. You sit down to a delicious meal with your family, and while talking about your day, you're reminded of God's deep and abiding compassion.

Day by day throughout Lent, you can see the Lord and experience his goodness if you know where to look. Every sacrifice, every act of charity, every moment of prayer is an opportunity to fully wake up to, and witness, the goodness of the Lord. As we walk through Lent and see who Jesus is, we can then be faithful to him day by day.

Pick a Challenge for this Week

- Instead of immediately grabbing your phone when you wake up each day, say a quick prayer. Ask the Lord to show you what he wants you to see and pay attention to that day.

- Give up watching your favorite TV show or YouTube channel this week. Every time you're tempted to watch it, take a walk or just look out a window for a while. Observe the natural world and thank God for what you see.

- Each evening, think of the most moving and challenging things you saw throughout the day and tell Jesus how those things influenced your heart and mind.

Feel Ambitious?

Read Luke 9:28–36 and then write down five thoughts you have about what Peter, James, and John saw on top of the mountain. Be honest about what you think and feel.

Closing Prayer

Jesus, open my eyes to see your glory,
and give me strength to walk with you.
Wake me to your goodness and comfort me
when I face the things that frighten me.
Amen.

Second Monday of Lent

I believe **I shall see the Lord's goodness**
in the land of the living.
—Psalm 27:13

You know this one: A glass sits on the counter, filled halfway. Is it half empty or half full? What's your first thought? Do you find yourself always seeing the emptiness in life, or the fullness? When we try to find even a fleeting glimpse of something positive, we're trying to see God because God *is* good. Striving to see goodness and letting ourselves be shaped by it, is the only way to keep our eyes focused on the prize: union with Christ.

Look for goodness *first* in the land of the living. That's what this desert is—a place for you to seek God in Christ Jesus.

Grow Your Soul

List three good things you saw recently. What made them good? Next to each one, give God a name that reflects that moment. For example, if you saw a child hug her dad, you might say, "God is love."

1.
2.
3.

Feel Ambitious?

Read Psalm 27:7–14 and talk to the Lord about any struggles you have seeing the good in your life.

Closing Prayer

Jesus, help me see your goodness.
Give me confidence that you will be by my side.
Open my eyes to you.
Amen.

Second Tuesday of Lent

Look upon me, have pity on me,
for I am alone and afflicted.
Relieve the troubles of my heart.
—Psalm 25:16–17

We can look for, and see, God in both big and small ways. You can see God in the sunrise, or hear God in the laugh of a friend. God also sees you. He sees when you're happy, rejoicing in the goodness you've experienced. And God sees when you're hurting—suffering at the hand of a friend or family member, struggling in school, or trying to find balance with all your commitments. God knows when you're longing to be included—when you feel alone, or ache with the pain of being misunderstood. God sees you. God looks and waits for you.

Being vulnerable is hard. But if we can muster the courage to let Jesus look upon us when we are hurting, to show him our wounds, he will heal us by standing beside us and holding us close to his heart. Our pain will ease, and our wounds will begin to heal.

Grow Your Soul

Write about a time when you felt alone and isolated. Why were you hurting? What did you do about it? Has that wound healed in full or in part? Take it to God in prayer.

Feel Ambitious?

Read Psalm 25:16–22 and ask the Lord to help you overcome the troubles of your heart.

Closing Prayer

Jesus, I want to be seen by you.
Look upon me and comfort me in my times of hurt.
Be with me when I feel most alone.
Amen.

Second Wednesday of Lent

For **you are my rock and my fortress**;
for your name's sake lead me and guide me.
—Psalm 31:4

Did you ever build a pillow fort as a kid, surrounding yourself with cushions and blankets, resting in the nooks and crannies of this squishy hideaway? The pillow fort was like a kingdom, a domain in which to hide toys, read books, store secrets, stay safe. It was a place of comfort and refuge.

God is a fortress for us—a place of comfort, safety, peace, rest, and protection. But that's not always easy to see. We're not always on top of a mountain looking at Jesus. Sometimes we're standing in the hall at school, feeling betrayed by a friend or having failed a test. Maybe our team just lost the big game. It's really hard to see God as a fortress in those moments. But just as we found refuge in living-room pillow forts, we can find safety and comfort in our God.

Grow Your Soul

Think of a moment from the past few days when you could have used God as your rock and fortress. What would it take for you to rely on him the next time a difficult situation comes along?

Feel Ambitious?

Read Psalm 31 and think about times when you've been hurt or distressed and asked the Lord for comfort. Thank the Lord for those times.

Closing Prayer

Jesus, I look for you when I'm hurt.
Give me peace and protection, comfort and rest.
Lead me and keep me safe.
Amen.

Second Thursday of Lent

He is like a tree planted near streams of water,
that yields its fruit in season.
—Psalm 1:3

When we were in kindergarten, we planted lima beans in clear plastic cups and watched them grow. Maybe you did too! Each day, we'd see the roots move a little deeper into the soil as the bean pod got a little bigger, preparing to sprout. It was fascinating to see how deeply the roots of that little bean went down into the dirt. This wasn't a mighty tree, but the roots were strong enough to keep that small sprout growing.

The Lord sets down deep roots too—in our hearts. We, in turn, become grounded in him. And then, eventually, we yield fruit. You can see how he grows within your heart, and how you grow as a result of him being in your life, sharing your successes and struggles. He is planted within your heart so that you can yield good fruit. Grow with Christ as he grows in you.

Grow Your Soul

Identify two ways you've seen yourself grow already this Lenten season, bearing fruit in your life. How have you been stretched and challenged by this walk with Jesus?

Feel Ambitious?

Read Psalm 1 and ask the Lord to open your mind to all the ways he has yielded fruit in your life.

Closing Prayer

Jesus, I want to be rooted in you.
I want to see you become rooted in me.
Show me how you are growing in my life,
and help me to keep growing.
Amen.

Second Friday of Lent

Give thanks to the Lord, invoke his name;
make known among the peoples his deeds!
—Psalm 105:1

There's nothing quite as special as sharing really good news. Parents put A+ tests on the fridge, athletes dance together in the end zone, friends text each other when they get a driver's license, a date to prom, or a scholarship to their first-choice college. We love to spread the good news stories of our lives because we want to share our joy with the people we love. And sometimes even with strangers.

What if we did that with the Good News of the Lord? What if we learn to tell other people about the things he's done, and how we've been changed by seeing him at work and growing in friendship with him? Do we keep Jesus to ourselves, or do we make him known to our friends, family, classmates, teachers, and even strangers?

Grow Your Soul

Name one or two situations where you've had the opportunity to share Jesus lately. Did you do so? If yes, did you use words or actions? If no, why did you hesitate?

Feel Ambitious?

Read Psalm 105:1–11 and reflect on ways you've already seen God make himself known to you this Lent.

Closing Prayer

Jesus, I want to share your goodness.
Give me courage to make you known
in my words and in my actions.
I love you, Lord.
Amen.

Second Saturday of Lent

Bless the Lord, my soul;
all my being, bless his holy name!
—Psalm 103:1

When we really see the Lord's goodness, we are changed forever. Whether standing on top of a mountain aware of his glory for the first time, or sitting in a classroom comforting an upset friend, we are constantly surrounded by the goodness, power, mercy, and love of our God. If we just pay attention, and open our eyes to see, then we become different. We are empowered by his goodness, aware of his movement in our lives. We learn to trust his plans, and what we see of the Lord allows us to be rooted in him.

This second week of Lent has been a time for you to practice seeing God and letting yourself be seen by him. You've noticed moments when you've had to trust him, identified opportunities you've had to share him, recognized times when you've felt unseen by others, and experienced instances when you've been able to cling to the heart of the Lord and find comfort in him. You are a new creation, because of what you've seen.

This Week's Wins

- Think back on your week and write down three Lenten exercises you did well. Where did you sacrifice? How did you pray? What did you give?

- What three things are you most grateful for at the end of this week?

- How did you see God act, and what stood out most to you?

Feel Ambitious?

Read the story of Joseph, son of Jacob, found in Genesis 37, 42–45. Write down some of the moments where God has brought good out of difficult times in your life. For example, did the death of a pet bring you closer to your siblings? Did tutoring sessions help you see that other students struggle with math, too?

Closing Prayer

Jesus, I want to see you fully,
know you completely, trust you entirely,
and be changed forever by your love.
Bless me fully and transform me.
Amen.

Third Sunday of Lent
CUT IT DOWN

> It may bear fruit in the future.
> If not, **you can cut it down**.
> —Luke 13:9

There are times in the gospels when Jesus speaks in such a way that we feel comforted and inspired. However, there are other passages that call us out, such as the gospel reading for this third Sunday of Lent. Both types of messages are important for followers of Jesus. It isn't easy to hear uncomfortable words, but we have to remember that Jesus didn't walk among us to tell us what we *want* to hear, but rather what we *need* to hear.

How often do you feel anxious or overwhelmed? How often do you feel like you're stumbling around, tripping over the same obstacles or flaws within yourself? Between school, work, and our social lives, it's a wonder that we even find a minute to catch our breath, let alone figure out how to be saintly, or even just a slightly better person. But Jesus invites us to examine our lives, to think about what gives us life and what doesn't. Then we need to act as wise and courageous gardeners, knowing which things to help grow and which things to cut down.

Pick a Challenge for this Week

- Each morning, think of one individual to show kindness to that day. Consider who in your life seems to need a confidence boost or who you might have some tension with that can be eased by kindness.

- On a sheet of paper, make three columns labeled *Fruit-bearing*, *Barren*, and *Fertilizer*. Each day write down your activities in the first two columns. If the activity brings you peace and joy, place it under

Fruit-bearing. If it drains you, place it under *Barren*. In the *Fertilizer* column, write one thing you can do to cultivate better outcomes for the things that are draining you, and one way you can maintain the activities that are bearing good fruit.

- Each evening, ask yourself: What did I see today that moved and challenged me? Tell Jesus how those things influenced your heart and mind.

Feel Ambitious?

Read Luke 13:1–9, and throughout the week, take time to reflect on the relationships in your life. Which ones are bearing good fruit and making you a better person? Which ones are barren, bringing out the worst in you? Come up with a fertilizer plan for the ones that are barren. What can be done to heal or enhance those relationships, or is it time to cut those negative influences out of your life?

Closing Prayer

Jesus, help me to view my life through your eyes.
Let me do only what brings me closer to you,
and give me strength to prune or cut out the things that don't.
Amen.

Third Monday of Lent

Surely, I wait for the Lord;
who bends down to me and hears my cry.
—Psalm 40:2

Sometimes we put up a wall and pretend everything is fine when, in fact, we are drained. This week, as we seek to revitalize parts of our lives that have grown stale or to cut down things that are draining us of joy, we first pause to recognize that we are in need of the Lord's help.

Christianity is not some glorified self-help program, and Lent is not the "Jesus version" of a forty-day cleanse. It is a time when Jesus invites us to take a good, long look at ourselves, and then asks us to change permanently so we can become more like him. This change is not immediate, and so we must imitate the psalmist and wait . . . patiently.

Grow Your Soul

Identify three things or relationships in your life that you know need to improve. Perhaps you want to be more organized and productive, maybe there is a broken friendship to mend, or maybe you want to stop gossiping. Ask Jesus to show you how you can change to become more like him.

1.
2.
3.

Feel Ambitious?

Read Psalm 40, and whenever the psalm uses a metaphor (pit of destruction, muddy clay, rock, etc.), write what that represents in your life. Be specific and personal.

Closing Prayer

Jesus, I am weak.
Give me the courage to cry out to you,
and the patience to wait for help. Amen.

Third Tuesday of Lent

My eyes are ever upon the Lord,
who frees my feet from the snare.
—Psalm 25:15

Have you ever experienced this? The day is going well, and then it suddenly gets derailed by some event, some person, some mistake, or even our own thoughts. And in our spiritual lives it can be even worse. As we strive to cultivate virtue, our progress can be slowed, or even reversed, by the maddening snare of sin. Most of our sins are the result of self-inflicted snares. We know a thing is bad for us, and yet for the sake of momentary pleasure, we jump in with both feet.

Rats don't eat rat poison because it tastes like poison. They eat it because it tastes good. We need to be better than rats, not seeking fleeting pleasure, but keeping our eyes focused on Jesus, striving to abound in everlasting joy . . . snare (and poison) free.

Grow Your Soul

Avoiding the pathway to sin is often easier than avoiding the sin directly. Write down a few of your habitual patterns of sin. Ask yourself: What triggers me to walk down that road? Stress? Lonliness? Anger? Fear?

Feel Ambitious?

Read Psalm 25:1–7. Jot down three sinful habits that you want to change. Next to them write down what you think the Lord would have you do instead.

Closing Prayer

Jesus, like a moth to a flame,
I am often drawn to things that bring me harm.
Free me from my snares and protect me.
Amen.

Third Wednesday of Lent

The Lord rebuilds Jerusalem,
and gathers the dispersed of Israel,
**Healing the brokenhearted,
and binding up their wounds**.
—Psalm 147:2–3

Take a breath. This week can be hard as we look to cut down the areas of sin in our lives. As we do this difficult yet necessary work, we need to remind ourselves that any guilt or pain is not meant for its own sake, or to last forever. Jesus' desire is always to heal and to transform.

When you lift weights, you create tiny tears in the muscles. But when your body recovers and those little tears heal, you are stronger than ever. Over the last few weeks, you've been making spiritual tears to build muscle and become strong in the Lord. Today, remind yourself to rest in the healing presence of God.

Grow Your Soul

Spend five minutes in silent prayer, meditating on Christ's desire to heal you. Write a list of the spiritual tears you've made so far this Lent, and how those have been transformative in your life.

Feel Ambitious?

Read Psalm 147 and schedule a time to go to Confession at your parish church, your school, or wherever it's available this Lent.

Closing Prayer

Jesus, my wounds are deep and many.
Help me to experience your mercy
and rest in your healing presence.
Amen.

Third Thursday of Lent

For he is our God,
we are the people he shepherds,
the sheep in his hands.
—Psalm 95:7

Ever wonder why the Bible uses the language of sheep and shepherd to help us comprehend our proper relationship to the Lord? It illustrates our need to trust God, since a shepherd knows how to protect and care for his sheep, and helps us curb our pride.

Sheep have no defense against predators and are mostly clueless about how to survive on their own; we need our Good Shepherd to protect us from evil and temptation. It is one thing for us to recognize that God exists, and acknowledge that we believe in, love, and want to follow Jesus. It is quite another to recognize and acknowledge that we *need* him.

Grow Your Soul

As an exercise in humility, identify three things that you don't know how to do well, or at all, but want to be able to do. These can be spiritual, academic, or even household tasks. Approach someone who knows how to do those things and ask them to help you learn.

Feel Ambitious?

Read Psalm 95 and think of something that you "need" to get through the day such as coffee or a cell phone. Just for today, go without it.

Closing Prayer

Jesus, my pride keeps me from following you.
Help me to become humble,
and trust you as a sheep trusts its shepherd.
Amen.

Third Friday of Lent

In distress you called and I rescued you;
I answered you in secret with thunder.
—Psalm 81:8

What are we supposed to do when we call out to God and there is no answer? If this is supposed to be a relationship, why does it feel like we're the only one talking? While feeling this way is completely understandable, we need to consider that we may be unable to hear God's voice because of the constant noise in our lives.

We love and serve a God who speaks in whispers and live in a world of constant clamor with social media, group texts, and every movie, TV show, and song available for instant streaming. It is time we take stock of the noise level in our lives and turn it down, so we can hear God.

Grow Your Soul

Choose to make one of the following sacrifices today:

- Do not listen to music today. Whenever you want to listen, pause for five minutes of silent prayer instead. Can you hear God whispering?
- Drop social media and texting for today. Instead, hang out with people in person.
- Spend twenty minutes in silence when you get home from school or work. Pray if you can, or just think about your life.

Feel Ambitious?

Read Psalm 81 and spend an hour in silent prayer with Jesus.

Closing Prayer

Jesus, my life is cluttered and noisy.
Help me to find silence and simplicity
that I may hear your still, small voice.
Amen.

Third Saturday of Lent

Restore to me the gladness of your salvation;
uphold me with a willing spirit.
—Psalm 51:14

Believe it or not, God doesn't desire for us to be miserable. Even in the midst of Lent, we are still an Easter people! And this week, as you cut things out of your life to make room for God, he has been present to you in big and small ways: in the smile shared between friends, in the giggle of an infant, in the simple activities that brought joy to your heart, in the silence you made time for, in the intentional sacrifices you made. Each moment was a chance to be restored to God's goodness and to cut things out that remove you from him.

This third week of Lent, you intentionally and purposefully got rid of things that have kept you from God in the past. You've made time to be reconciled to God, you've given yourself a chance to be quiet and listen to his voice, and you've looked at what really does prevent you from growing close to the One who loves you most. God knows us better than we know ourselves, and he knows what you've needed to cut out and remove. This week was a chance to work with him to do that, and to let God show you where he is, what's kept you from him, and how you can be joyfully restored to a relationship with him.

This Week's Wins

•   Were there any barren areas that produced fruit this week? How and why? What did you do differently?

- Which snares did you successfully avoid? What repeat sins have you begun working on overcoming?

- Did you experience any moments of peace? When? What was that like?

Feel Ambitious?

Read Psalm 51:11–19 and think about something you do that brings you joy. Invite God to spend time with you while you're doing it. Make it your prayer.

Closing Prayer

Jesus, you called the first disciples while they were fishing.
Help me find you in the everyday activities of my life.
Amen.

Fourth Sunday of Lent
GET FOUND

But now we must celebrate and rejoice,
because your brother was dead and has come to life again;
he was lost and has been found.
—Luke 15:32

The story of the Prodigal Son is familiar, not just because we hear it regularly, but because we've each lived it in some way. We ask for what we think is rightfully ours, waste the riches given to us, and come back with our heads hung low. What's most important is how we're met when we return: we're welcomed home.

In the midst of our Lenten journey, we may be tempted to hide the dead and lost parts of ourselves from Jesus—the parts of ourselves we've squandered and wasted. We may think Jesus will see how messy we actually are and say, "Thanks, but no thanks." But, if we truly wish to follow and walk with Jesus, we must understand and embrace this fundamental truth: when we are at our worst, Jesus still wants us. He wants us to let him in, even when we waste the goodness we've been given.

In order for every part of us that was dead to be made alive, and all that was lost in us to be found again, all of it must be united to Christ. We must allow ourselves to be fully seen by—and be fully with—him. There's no need to hide. It's time to come home, and get found.

Pick a Challenge for this Week

- When you wake up each morning, think of something you've been trying to hide from Jesus. Name it. And offer it to him for healing.

- Make a list of people that you have offended, hurt, abandoned, or said mean things about. Make time to have a conversation with each of them this week, apologize for what you've done, and ask for their forgiveness.

• Find a prayer book or online resource that helps you examine your conscience. Ask yourself: What parts of my life feel dead or lost? Take that list to Confession at some point this week, and approach Jesus for healing and forgiveness.

Feel Ambitious?

Read Luke 15:1–3, 11–32, the story of the Prodigal Son. Make a list of moments when you've felt welcomed home by Jesus.

Closing Prayer

Jesus, at times I feel lost and undeserving of your love.
Give me the courage to return home to you.
Amen.

Fourth Monday of Lent

You changed my mourning into dancing;
you took off my sackcloth
and clothed me with gladness.
—Psalm 30:12

Forgiveness is a tricky thing. It can be difficult to give, especially when we've been deeply wounded or when the one who hurt us hasn't admitted fault or apologized. It's also sometimes hard to accept forgiveness when we have deeply wounded another.

The guilt we feel for the evil we have done, and the good we have failed to do, is real. It should drive us to Confession. But if we are not careful, guilt can affect us so profoundly that we start thinking we are beyond God's power to forgive and heal us. We may begin to wonder if God can really love us. When those fears come, we need to remember that God's forgiveness is complete. Forgive yourself, make amends, and let it go. Once he has forgiven you, God doesn't hold it over your head waiting for repayment. God forgives out of love. Don't hide in your guilt. Touch God's mercy, and be at peace.

Grow Your Soul

Journal about this question: What part of you does God most delight in?

Feel Ambitious?

Read Psalm 30 and think about the last year, month, or week of your life. Write down areas where you have grown or been transformed.

Closing Prayer

Jesus, I sometimes feel as if you could never love me.
Help me to experience your love and grace.
Turn my darkness into light and sadness into joy.
Amen.

Fourth Tuesday of Lent

Turn from evil and do good;
seek peace and pursue it.
—Psalm 34:15

As we walk this Lenten journey, it's important to be mindful of our travel companions and how we treat them as we go. Undoubtedly, there will be days when you come across someone with whom you disagree or who annoys you. Conflicts are unavoidable and can lead to real growth.

In an argument, we may discover that the other person has some valid points. But rather than acknowledge this and seek common ground, we dig our heels in and escalate the tension. Or we may be locked in a battle to change someone's opinion or a behavior of theirs that we find frustrating. In these moments, ask, "Do I want to be happy, or do I want to be right?" While being right may please you, the path to peace is forged by choosing the former. In order for the image of God to be found in us by a stranger, friend, or enemy, we must pursue peace.

Grow Your Soul

Write down the names of the three people who most annoy you. For each person, recall a moment when you have seen the image of God in them, and ask the Lord to soften your heart toward them.

Feel Ambitious?

Read Psalm 34 and reflect on the overall state of your immediate family. What can you do to seek peace in your house?

Closing Prayer

Jesus, I often let my need to be right
prevent me from seeing you in others.
Prince of Peace, help me bring your peace to my world.
Amen.

Fourth Wednesday of Lent

The Lord is near to all who call upon him,
to all who call upon him in truth.
—Psalm 145:18

God is really bad at hide-and-seek. He is hidden in everything, but easily found. But why does it seem at times so incredibly hard to find God?

Many of us have been left frustrated by trying, and failing, to feel God's presence in others or the world around us. At times we have looked for God without first opening our eyes. Sometimes we are blinded by the flawed or distorted view we have of ourselves. This is precisely why God has hidden himself in all things. Even if we merely stumble upon him, he will lead us from self-deception to self-awareness. We will see ourselves as much-loved children of God, for once we find God, we find our true selves.

Grow Your Soul

Write down the things you love most about your family members (your mom, dad, brothers and sisters, grandparents, cousins). Be specific. What do you find delightful about them? At some point today, share what you wrote with one or two of them.

Feel Ambitious?

Read Psalm 145 and think about (and maybe journal about) where you may have encountered God recently, even if you weren't fully aware of it at the time. Look for hints in this psalm, which describes the attributes of God.

Closing Prayer

Jesus, give me eyes to see you, ears to hear you,
a mind that seeks you in all things,
and a heart that loves you always.
Amen.

Fourth Thursday of Lent

Remember me, Lord, as you favor your people;
come to me with your saving help.
—Psalm 106:4

Life can be intimidating. Through the media we consume or the observations of our own family and friends, we may look at the giftedness or accomplishments of others and begin to feel very small. On its own, that's not necessarily a bad thing. It is good to keep our pride in check by recognizing that the world does not revolve around us. But often, we freeze-frame someone when they are at their best and compare ourselves to them when we are at our worst.

Rather than constantly measuring ourselves against others, we need to take a moment to look only at ourselves and the gifts we have to offer the world. Go find a need in this world that your gifts can meet! If you don't know what your gifts are, or if you think you don't have any, go and serve God's people, and you will find your gift.

Grow Your Soul

Clean up after your friends at lunch today. Pick up their trash; turn in their cafeteria trays. Do it without expecting anything in return.

Feel Ambitious?

Read Psalm 106 and reflect on one of your God-given gifts. Come up with a plan for how to use that gift to serve others over the next few days.

Closing Prayer

Jesus, show me how to show favor to your people,
and to serve others out of the gifts you have given me.
Help me to humbly seek to serve you.
Amen.

Fourth Friday of Lent

Look to him and be radiant,
and your faces may not blush for shame.
—Psalm 34:6

We all have that one friend—the one who only texts when they want something from us, or when their life is filled with drama. A relationship with that person can be emotionally draining and devoid of joy. Sometimes we can be that person to others, and sadly, for many of us, we are that person with God. We only pray when we want something or run to church when bad things happen.

Mercifully, God does not grow tired of us even when we take him for granted. But, if we treat God like this forever, *we* will be the ones who grow weary, frustrated, and joyless. God is not a concept, but a person, so in order to find the love and joy of the Lord, we must give ourselves the space and opportunity to speak in praise of him. Not just about what he's done for us, but about who he is and how he loves us.

Grow Your Soul

Name all the things you love about God and your relationship with him. Think of a song that represents your current relationship with God and use that song in a prayer today.

Feel Ambitious?

Read Psalm 34 and have a conversation with your parents or a couple that you know. Have them tell you what they love most about each other.

Closing Prayer

Jesus, at times my relationship with you feels stale.
Remind me of who you are
so that I may fall in love with you all over again.
Help me to share that love with others.
Amen.

Fourth Saturday of Lent

I will thank the Lord in accordance with his justice;
I will sing the name of the Lord Most High.
—Psalm 7:18

There are days when the stars seem to align and all things fall into place. We have energy, focus, drive, and contentment. We are on top of our game, and everything is as it should be. On other days, we feel lethargic, agitated, or discontented. We lose interest in our relationships, responsibilities, and the mundane activities of everyday life. Quite simply, we get in a funk.

This ebb and flow is also true of the spiritual life. There are moments when we wouldn't be surprised if we could reach out our hand to touch heaven's gates! And then there are moments when our prayers bounce off the ceiling and we feel utterly alone. While the moments of dryness and dullness are concerning, they are totally normal, natural, and even necessary, because it's in these moments that we have the potential to grow the most.

When you feel lost and alone, looking for a way out, remember God's graciousness, and give thanks. Be thankful for the small blessings of food and shelter. Be thankful for the big blessings of love, family, and friendships. Be thankful for the times you have been delivered from the storms of your past.

This Week's Wins

- Did you make it to Confession this week? If so, what were you cleansed of? If not, what stopped you?

- What did you discover about yourself, others, or God this week? Where? How? How will those discoveries change you?

- In what ways did you serve others? How did serving others make you feel?

Feel Ambitious?

Read Psalm 7 and reflect on the past week. Name all the things you can recall that you are thankful for. Give God praise!

Closing Prayer

Jesus, I often focus on my storms and not my Savior.
Help me to remember your kindness,
and that you will never abandon me.
Amen.

Fifth Sunday of Lent
LIVE MERCY

Let **the one among you who is without sin**
be the first to throw a stone.
—John 8:7

The story of the woman caught in adultery (John 8:1–11) clearly illustrates how God sees and loves sinners, and how he calls us to do the same.

A woman caught in adultery is brought before Jesus, and the religous authorities ask Jesus how to respond—the standard punishment for that crime was being stoned to death. He does what he always does, with every sinner: he saves her. But he does it by telling the crowd they are free to kill her, provided they have never sinned themselves. They, of course, leave, and Jesus forgives the woman and tells her to sin no more.

We're not called to turn a blind eye to destructive and sinful behaviors. Jesus acknowledges the woman's sin but then offers her a new life. He takes the long view and recognizes that she is way more than this one sin. Sinful actions don't exist in isolation. They arise as individual pieces of a much larger story. To live mercy is to see that bigger story, enter into it, and help write a better one—for others and for ourselves.

Pick a Challenge for this Week:

- Each morning, pray this simple prayer before you get out of bed: "Lord Jesus, help me see others with the eyes of mercy and forgiveness. Help me approach you for mercy and forgiveness in my life." Think of one person to forgive or from whom you will seek forgiveness this week.

- Give up your favorite snack, soda, or food this week. Every time you want to eat or drink it, say a simple prayer for those who are stuck in habitual sins that lead them away from Jesus.

- Each evening, think about all the ways you saw God's mercy throughout the day, whether by receiving it or by sharing it with others. Keep a list of each moment you remember to reflect on at week's end.

Feel Ambitious?

Read John 8:1–11 and reflect on your life and relationships through the lens of the passage. Write down times when you have been in the position of the crowd, the woman, and Jesus. How did you respond in each situation? Did you do the right thing? If not, how will you seek forgiveness?

Closing Prayer

Jesus, help me see beyond the failings of others.
Show me how to help them write a better story.
Reveal to me your merciful ways.
Amen.

Fifth Monday of Lent

Indeed, **goodness and mercy will pursue me**
all the days of my life.
—Psalm 23:6

Keep your eyes open, because you are being pursued. As the psalmist points out, God's goodness and mercy pursue us throughout our lives. Certainly God showers these gifts on us and assures us forgiveness when we falter. But this pursuit also means we are compelled to shower goodness and mercy on others. These gifts constantly prod us to be shared.

When you walk into the cafeteria and you see that one kid who always seems out of place, do you ever invite him to sit with you and your friends? Or do you shrug your shoulders and act like it isn't your problem? When you're sitting in class and a few of your fellow students once again pick on or laugh at everyone's favorite punching bag, do you defend her, or at the very least distract the mocking crowd, or do you shrink in your desk and pretend to study?

Do we give what we receive? Do you shower goodness and mercy on those around you all the days of your life? God asks no less.

Grow Your Soul

Today, try to find three moments that provide you an opportunity to extend goodness and mercy to others. How will you take advantage of those moments to show God's love?

Feel Ambitious?

Read Psalm 23 and reflect on the times you have been shown mercy and goodness by others. Find a way to thank those people.

Closing Prayer

Jesus, open my heart to your goodness and mercy,
and teach me to share these gifts with all whom I meet.
Amen.

Fifth Tuesday of Lent

The Lord looked down from the holy heights,
viewed the earth from heaven,
To attend to the groaning of the prisoners,
to release those doomed to die.
—Psalm 102:20–21

While we rejoice in the notion of God setting captives free, most of us will never feel the cold steel of handcuffs or the isolation of a jail cell. However, we may be imprisoned by our fear of the unknown, of failure, rejection, or loneliness. We may be shackled by anxiety or held hostage by hatred, laziness, or pain from our past.

What has given you comfort in, or freedom from, your imprisonment? Encouragement from a loved one? An act of kindness by a stranger? Perhaps you were given the chance to contribute to something and share your talents. Extend the gift of mercy today by offering relief to someone whose heart is groaning. Help set them free.

Grow Your Soul

Think of someone who has deeply wounded you. Ask God to help you forgive them and set your spirit free. Then find a way to let that person know you have forgiven them.

Feel Ambitious?

Read Psalm 102:13–29 and offer a brief, spontaneous prayer for prisoners, that their hearts may be free. Consider joining the Dismas Ministry Union of Prayer to support those working in prison ministry: https://dismasministry.org/union-of-prayer.

Closing Prayer

Jesus, the chains that bind me are the ones I won't let go.
Release me from my prisons
so I can bring your freedom to others. Amen.

Fifth Wednesday of Lent

Then **our mouths were filled with laughter;
our tongues sang for joy**.
Then it was said among the nations,
"The Lord had done great things for them."
—Psalm 126:2

Faith is serious business, but we cannot forget that the joy of the Lord is our strength. How often do you walk into church and think, "Wow, everyone seems so happy!" Too often the practice of our religion seems to bring somber moods at best and at worst tension and division.

If Jesus came so that we might live life to the fullest, then experiencing and spreading the fullness of joy needs to be a core value of our identity as followers of Jesus. A shared smile or a joke to break the tension is not only good for that moment and time; a positive encounter can turn someone's day, month, or even life around. Now is the time for us who are seeking to live mercy to get to work and be joyful.

Grow Your Soul

Try to make two or three people laugh today (without dissing someone or something). At the end of the day, write down who they were, how you made them laugh, and how doing so made you feel.

Feel Ambitious?

Read Psalm 126 and journal about things that make you laugh. For each thing, ask yourself: Why does this bring me joy? How can I seek more of it in my day-to-day life?

Closing Prayer

*Jesus, our world is full of anger and bitterness.
Help me be a light in the darkness,
and spread joy wherever I can.
Amen.*

Fifth Thursday of Lent

He has not dealt with us as our sins merit,
nor requited us as our wrongs deserve.
—Psalm 103:10

Mercy is something that we love to receive but are reluctant to give. When we have wronged others, we often generate a quick list of reasons to justify what we've done, or at least alleviate the seriousness of the offense. But of course we are all capable of being selfish, ignorant, and hateful. Yet God has not cast us out, punishing us with anger. In fact, he draws even closer to heal and redeem us.

Live mercy this week by imitating our heavenly Father. Treat those who have wronged you in the same manner God has treated you: show them mercy, forgiveness, and abundant kindness.

Grow Your Soul

Think about the person who annoys you the most in your daily life, and do something kind for them today, such as bringing them a breakfst treat or giving them a compliment.

Feel Ambitious?

Read Psalm 103 and think about the worst thing you've done to someone. If that had been done to you, how would you have responded? Journal about your thoughts and feelings and ask God to show you how to be more merciful.

Closing Prayer

*Jesus, I am sorry for the times I have kept your gifts
of mercy and forgiveness to myself,
and burdened others with guilt.
Help me to forgive what seems unforgivable,
and to love the unlovable.
Amen.*

Fifth Friday of Lent

Sing to the Lord, praise the Lord,
For **he has rescued the life of the poor,
from the power of the evildoers**!
—Jeremiah 20:13

Serving the poor is something we as Catholics know we're supposed to do. Many times we respond to this mandate of our faith by helping sort cans for food drives, or putting a few dollars in the Salvation Army bucket at Christmastime. But we remain mostly at arm's length from real poverty. Or do we?

It's likely that some of your classmates are poor in academics, in friendship, or in confidence. The ways we can serve these people are simple: offering a few study tips or help with homework, sitting with them at lunch when they might otherwise eat alone, or complimenting those who seem to lack confidence.

Serving the poor might mean responding to needs right in front of you every day. It's not only about giving to those with financial and material need. It is also about serving those closest to us.

Grow Your Soul

Think about one person at school or in your family who is in need right now. Choose one action to take to address that person's poverty.

Feel Ambitious?

Read Jeremiah 20. Take any money you would spend on yourself this weekend and instead buy something for a friend or family member.

Closing Prayer

Jesus, you spent your life with the poor and destitute.
Help me to see your face in the poor.
Show me where I can serve you today.
Amen.

Fifth Saturday of Lent

With age-old love I have loved you;
so I have kept my mercy toward you.
—Jeremiah 31:3

Babies scream and cry when they are discontented. They don't know what's wrong, and even if they do, they don't have the language to express it. So they cry, trusting that Mom or Dad will know what to do.

We must never forget that we are, and always will be, children of God. So, when we are stressed or angry, frustrated or scared, angry or feeling alone and maybe confused—even if we don't know just how we feel—we can cry out to our God and trust that he will know what to do and will love us with an age-old, perfect, parental love.

Imagine you have a clean slate with another person, and you set out to love them more and better than anyone else. How would you treat them? What if they made a mistake, or even knowingly hurt you? Would loving them best mean shunning them forever, or would something deep inside stir you to forgive and care for them?

In the moments when our pride is wounded and our temper flares up against another, we must call to mind the age-old love of God, and show mercy to those who have hurt us.

This Week's Wins

- Did you forgive anyone this week? Did you seek forgiveness from anyone? What was that like?

- Did you spread joy to your friends and family? How? What was that like?

- Were you more understanding and forgiving to your friends, family, classmates, teammates, or even strangers? What can you do to keep a merciful and loving attitude to others?

Feel Ambitious?

Read Jeremiah 31 and spend some time praying through the following questions: Who in your life has loved you the most? How did they show this love to you? Who can you imagine loving in this way?

Closing Prayer

Jesus, help me trust you like a baby trusts her parents.
Help me love others the way you love me, perfectly and completely.
Give me patience with myself and those around me.
Amen.

Palm Sunday
TAKE AND EAT

Then he took the bread, said the blessing,
broke it, and gave it to them,
saying, "This is my body, which will be given for you;
do this in memory of me."
—Luke 22:19

We have finally come to the holiest week of the year. This is the week that gives all of our suffering and sacrifices meaning and value. In our worship this week we remember Jesus being welcomed with palm branches, flipping over tables in the Temple, being betrayed by a friend, instituting the Eucharist, saying goodbye to his closest friends, praying so hard he bleeds, and finally defeating sin and death by his Cross and Resurrection. There is so much to encounter and process this week, and you can be part of it each step of the way.

It can be intimidating, but the beauty of this week is that Christ and his Church invite you to not just read about things that happened long ago, but to walk alongside Jesus and experience each moment with him. The events we commemorate this week happened thousands of years ago in the Middle East, but this week they echo across time and fill us with new life. During Holy Week we die with Christ, so that on Easter Sunday we may rise anew with him. Do this in memory of him.

Pick a Challenge for this Week

*   Pray through two of the fourteen Stations of the Cross each day this week. Ask the Lord to reveal the mystery of his immense love to you as you contemplate his carrying of the Cross.

- Make a list of moments when you've felt pain—physical, spiritual, or emotional. Ask the Lord to heal you of any lingering sorrow or pain.

- Before watching any television this week, read the daily Mass readings (found on USCCB.org) and spend time meditating and praying about what you take from them.

Feel Ambitious?

Read Luke 22–23 and make plans to attend all of the Triduum services at your parish if possible.

Closing Prayer

Jesus, allow me to walk with you as you carry your Cross,
so I may learn how to carry my own
and find new life in you.
Amen.

Monday of Holy Week

Father, forgive them,
they know not what they do.
—Luke 23:34

Have you ever been caught ranting about something a friend did that annoyed you? Perhaps the person overheard your complaints to someone else. You may even be good friends with that person, but you are taking a moment to vent about them. Or maybe the reverse has happened, and you've caught a friend talking about you behind your back. Whichever side of this you happen to be on, there is pain. This wound is deep, even though it's very rarely an intentional one.

As Holy Week begins, give those who have wronged you the benefit of the doubt. Perhaps they simply didn't know what they were doing, and even if they did, they deserve to be reminded of the love and mercy of Christ. So forgive them and look for ways to love them, just as Jesus forgave and loved even those who put him to death.

Grow Your Soul

Who in your life has most severely hurt you? Pray that you can forgive that person and ask Jesus to help you find a way to heal. You may never completely mend the relationship, but God can mend your heart.

Feel Ambitious?

Write a letter to someone you've hurt, and apologize for what you did. Ask their forgiveness.

Closing Prayer

Jesus, I have hurt people, and I have been hurt.
Give me your patience and mercy to love those who harm me.
Give me your kindness and compassion to not hurt others.
I want to be forgiven, and I want to forgive.
Amen.

Tuesday of Holy Week

Amen, I say to you,
today you will be with me in Paradise.
—Luke 23:43

How often do you plan out the next day, week, year, or decade of your life? Most of us have dreams, if not expectations, about how our lives will go. But most of us have also felt the sting of something not going our way.

The good thief on the cross probably didn't dream that his life would end with him gasping for breath, crucified next to the Son of God. But, with his last breaths, he defends Jesus and whispers, "Remember me." And Jesus promises him paradise.

What is the honest, simple, core desire of your heart? In the midst of a life that often won't go your way, go to Jesus; if you befriend him and follow him, you will be with him one day in paradise.

Grow Your Soul

Write a letter to Jesus telling him what it is that you want most, right now in your life. Even if you think it cannot happen, revealing your deepest desires can open your heart and mind to new possibilities.

Feel Ambitious?

Do a little research into various understandings of paradise. Then journal or just spend time reflecting on how you think of paradise or heaven. Ask yourself: In what ways am I letting Jesus lead me to paradise?

Closing Prayer

Jesus, remember me.
When I'm tired, lonely, afraid, and worried.
When I fail, mess up, walk away from you, and stumble.
When I'm with my friends, family, and even my enemies.
And help me to always remember you. Amen.

Wednesday of Holy Week

When Jesus saw his mother
and the disciple there whom he loved,
he said to his mother, "Woman, behold, your son."
Then he said to the disciple, "**Behold, your mother**."
—John 19:26–27

There is no one in the history of humanity who is as close to the heart of Christ as his mother, Mary. From the Cross, Jesus offered to his beloved disciple John and to his mother the mutual care of one another as they witnessed his Passion. Christ offers the same to us. Mary, the first disciple, is to be for us a shining model of following the way of her Son, our Lord and Savior, Jesus. And she is to be our mother, tender and strong, compassionate while asking us to do and be our best.

It is worth noting that on Christ's *worst* day, he sought to entrust the care and protection of his mother to one of his closest friends. Today, Mary is your mother too. So, behold your Blessed Mother, and love her as Jesus loves her.

Grow Your Soul

Make a list of a few qualities of your mother (or a mother figure in your life) that you really value and admire. Share these things with her and tell her you appreciate what she's done for you in your life.

Feel Ambitious?

Pray a Rosary today for all the mother figures in your life. If you don't know how to pray the Rosary, ask a friend or do a quick internet search.

Closing Prayer

Jesus, give me the strength to look upon you as your mother did,
with eyes of love, adoration, admiration, and joy.
Help me turn to my own mother in times of need,
and trust your mother with my heart. Amen.

Holy Thursday

I **thirst**.
—John 19:28

When was the last time you asked for help? When was the last time you allowed someone to see you weak? When have you shown someone you are limited and not always perfect? We can so easily get caught up in the charade of trying to convince everyone that we always have it all together. Depending on who we're with, or what we're doing, we often hide behind masks of self-sufficiency. We don't want people to see us make a mistake, or fail, or be vulnerable.

But from the Cross, Jesus beckons us to take off our masks. He admits he needs relief—he tells those nearby that he thirsts. In doing so, he tells us that he thirsts for us to come to him, as we are, in our brokenness and with our own thirsts, with our mistakes, in our messes, and find relief in him.

Grow Your Soul

Make a list of two or three things you need help with. Who can you go to? Who can help you? Seek them out, admit your needs, your thirsts, and ask for help.

Feel Ambitious?

Pay attention to the people you're surrounded by every day. Ask yourself what they might need. How can you offer relief from those needs? Try to help three or four people today in significant ways. Even if what you offer brings little relief, you are sharing God's mercy.

Closing Prayer

Jesus, you were thirsty and needed help.
Help me acknowledge when I need you, and others,
and let me be unafraid to seek aid. Amen.

Good Friday

It is **finished**.
—John 19:30

It wasn't supposed to be like this—or so many people thought. For Jesus to be the Messiah, he should have come to set captives free, not become a prisoner himself. He came to usher in the kingdom of God, overthrow the Roman Empire, not die by crucifixion like a common criminal. And yet this is how salvation came.

Jesus' last words, "It is finished," are not the defeated gasp of a dying man, but the first roars of victory. God shows us that the image of triumph is not one of a conquering hero, but one of a suffocating Jew, writhing in pain on a cross.

This is indeed the Good News, because whatever struggles and storms we face, we can cling to two things: darkness and death are not the end of the story, and the battles being waged inside our very souls have already been won. Sin and death have been defeated by Jesus.

Grow Your Soul

Think about when you've felt defeated. How did you handle that feeling of defeat? Did you give up? What are some ways you can trust Jesus more to help you when you're down?

Feel Ambitious?

What sin or sorrow has been your greatest struggle since last Good Friday? Sit in prayer and hold that wound in your hand. Tell Jesus how you feel about it. When you feel ready, slowly open your hand and ask Jesus to take that struggle and replace it with new life.

Closing Prayer

Jesus, help me rely on you when I hurt.
Show me the goodness of what's to come,
and the beginning of the work you've done in my life. Amen.

Holy Saturday

After he had taken the body down,
**he wrapped it in a linen cloth and
laid him in a rock-hewn tomb**
in which no one had yet been buried.
—Luke 23:53

There's no washing of feet today. The Cross isn't venerated. It's quiet. There's no hustle and bustle. With the Eucharist gone, something about the church building feels off. There's an emptiness to everything.

It's enough to make us wonder: why don't we skip the "Holy" part and just call it Saturday? But if we do that, we're dismissing something hugely important.

Today is the day when Jesus went into hell itself and brought souls to heaven. He defeated sin and death, and that's a victory not just for those of us who were yet to come, but for everyone who ever existed up to that point. This is a big deal. Those in darkness saw a great light, as indeed the Light of Lights broke into total darkness and cast it out.

This Lenten journey has given us many ways to engage our thoughts and actions, so that we can glorify the Lord with our lives. We've explored the depths of our soul; made changes to draw closer to Jesus; spent time with people, showing them mercy and love; and examined ways we can trust the Lord more, pray more intensely, and seek his heart. There's tremendous value in the work we've done in this desert, but we're about to leave it, and a lot of the pitfalls and frustrations and struggles of life are waiting for us beyond this journey.

So on this *final* day before Easter—this Holy Saturday—we remember that Christ is always working in and through all things, at all times, to unite us to himself. We may see only a tomb, but we know it'll be empty soon. We've gone through the desert, and we're about to enter the garden of the Resurrection.

This Week's Wins

- Make a list of the five best things about your Lenten experience. Why were they good? What happened to you to make them important?

- Which day of Holy Week has been most powerful for you? Why? What did you find to be life-changing about that particular day?

- How can you live Lent throughout the year? Come up with an action plan to continue to pray, sacrifice, and serve.

Feel Ambitious?

Write a letter to yourself to read at the beginning of Lent *next* year. Reflect on what you experienced on this journey and tell yourself what you need to do to make it just as good, and fruitful, next year.

Closing Prayer

Jesus, thank you for this journey.
Thank you for inviting me into the desert,
for walking with me there,
and for transforming me along the way.
I love you, Lord. Amen.